GODDESS

GODDESS

And sometimes when I feel the passion
Feel the fire under my feet
Those small embers burning brighter as each second passes
My body races my mind to write down the verses
That my mind so carefully creates
Creations so carefully handcrafted
Yet leaving an unravelled soul in my wake
I search to find what my mind has written
What my mind has told my delicate hands to write with blisters
And as I scramble to grasp the words that make sense to me
I realize I will never know what my heart is screaming to me
Until I put down the pen and read

-Let me taste the words of my own as if I was a stranger to them

To all the women who have had their light stolen by
someone, including themselves

May you find it again,
burning brighter than you ever thought it could

CONTENTS

THIS PITY

Tell me again how I tainted my own name
With the choices and actions I've made
Tell me how you are speaking of me
As if I told you that's how I want to be identified

But I'll also tell you
How you have made me feel shame from something
I never felt shameful about

This Pity

Whistle at me again
And then yell something absurd
Rev your engine as you pass by like you think you're revving mine
Get your buds to help you construct tantalizing words
And get mad when I don't react
Keep saying *hey baby* until I respond
Because you think I'm going for the chase
Tell me I'm ugly and that you were joking when I turn you down
I've asked you to do all these things for no other reason than
I am a woman

-my eyerolls are welcome here

What was she wearing?
Say it again

Say it again louder so the people in the back can hear you
So we can all grab each others hands and become intertwined
Like vines of ivy
To encircle you
And stitch your mouth closed
For who gave you the courage to speak on behalf of others
Like it was her fault in *the beginning*
And during
And after

Slut.

Whore.
Thirsty.
Bitch.
Any word that has the power
To shame
To hurt
Someone else
Should not have the power to
Brand you
With
Their simple
Words

-And she will take it all back some day

Goddess

And there will be times when boys are not nice
They will open their lips and tell grand stories full of lies
They will be about you
And about what you did
Even though
Maybe
You never really did
They will embroider a bright letter for you to wear on your chest
Scarlet will be the colour
There will be times when boys are not nice
And they will try to convince the world of who you are
This is the moment it's up to you
Take that capital A and sew it to your chest
And turn the lies into something you are proud of
So make it your best

-My scarlet letter

This Pity

I've tasted the best
And found the worst
All in the same hands that held me

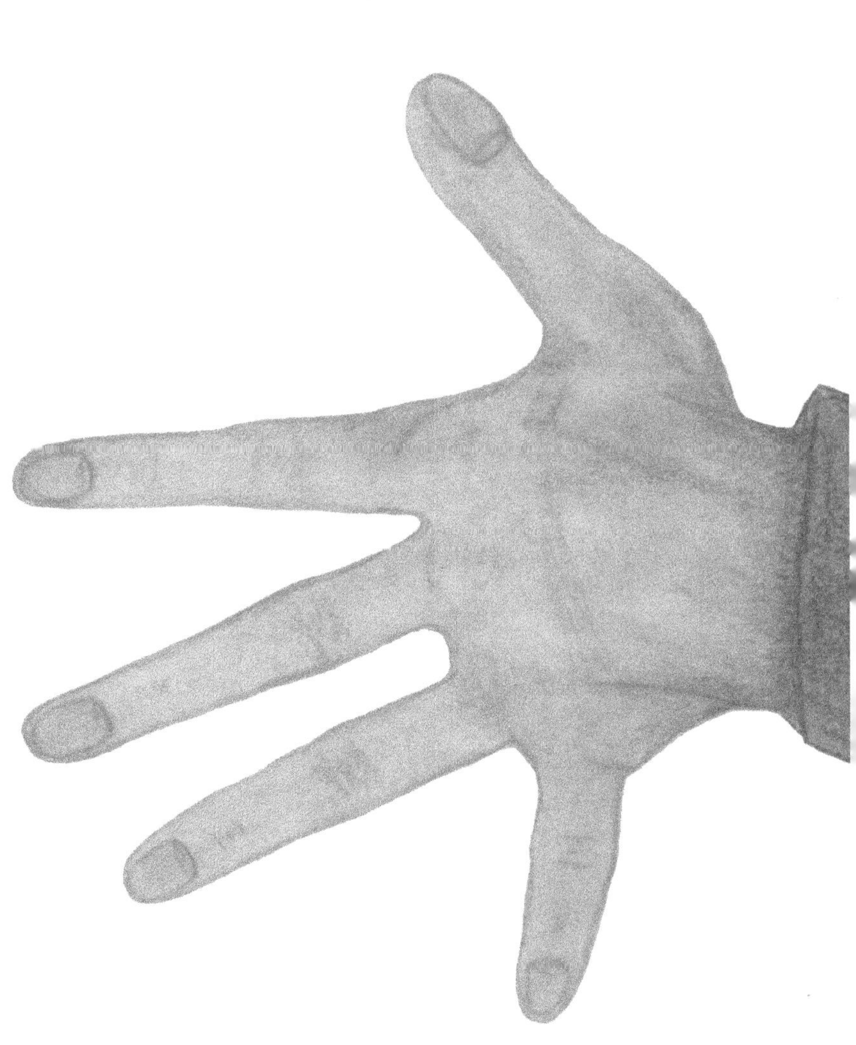

You carry hurt within your heart
Tied up with a delicate bow
Your intrigue leaves you tempted
But you don't want to travel this road again
He's funny, cute and sweet
The three red flags you call a cheat
Don't be afraid of him
He's not the one who broke you
So until the day he hurts you
Love him
Or at least give him the chance to love
And be loved by you

This Pity

I never knew it wasn't there until I noticed
We were laughing, like we always did
And you were smiling at me, the way you always had
But then I noticed

Where was it?
Was it there before and now it's gone?
Was it ever there?
I find myself searching his eyes, but it's scarce
I can't find it

I wasn't searching for a spark
I was searching for the look of love
The nameless expression of love in it's truest form
Unable to hide itself
Unable to do anything other than love

But it wasn't there
I couldn't find it

-love behind the eyes

Her beauty
Is your defeat
For all this attention
Makes you weak
She always loved you
But you were unsure
You closed off your heart
As your eyes
They blurred
She tried to convince you
But she knew the truth
You'd never be able to fully love her
Because you couldn't even love you

This Pity

They hand parts of themselves to those in need
For more selfish reasons than giving up greed
To put a smile on another's face and to give them one too
No harm in that
Really it's true
Though the motives turn their thin blood thick like butter
So that if someone ever asked they could have something sweet to utter
That they give to them and give not to get
Just to taste those warm words like sun on a baseball cap
They labelled themselves givers
Sewn on tight like a badge
Just so they could call themselves that

Your matches were wet
They helped you light your wick
But darling, they only did that
So they could be the one to *blow out your flame*

This Pity

As the tide rolled in and stayed in my path for a few moments longer
Than usual
I felt the pain deep within my soul
No tears
Just the acknowledgment that it was there
Like the almost sudden feeling of warm feet in cold water
It hit me
I didn't care if the sun was rising
If it was falling and setting
I just knew that this moment was for the pain
That wanted me to know was still there
Still in my core, though dormant for awhile
It did not want me to forget it
The emptiness, yet
A total pit of hurt carried in my ribcage as if pounding to be released
Knowing
The simple flow of water down my cheeks won't change a thing
I must wait for this tide to roll out
And be carried away with the currents
To let the deafening silence consume my thoughts
And swallow my hurt all over again

-Until next time, tide. I'll be awaiting your next visit

Goddess

And I look back to all the times
All the times we shared
Good and bad
I review in my mind when we tore apart
And how my heart broke
I would've sworn in two
And how I believed, truly
I'd never be okay, I'd never get over you
But here I sat and wrote about you still
About how I either still loved you
Or how I knew I would be okay eventually
Or how I'd write pretending I was
But now I laugh because I grew stronger
With everyday I tried forgetting you
And my mind became stronger too
For it was harder trying to let it's memories go
But now I smile because
Unlike all those other words I wrote time and time again
This time I have moved on
I can accept what was and what will be
And I admire how strong my mind could be
And is
Because, to date
This was the hardest thing I've had to let my anxiety release
Thank you for letting me unlove you

-In the ways I once did

And I saw the blue in him
But I was never talking about the colour

Identity

Crisp and colourful, leaves strewn on the ground
Lost was a charm she wish could be found
It used to be shiny, though now it's dull and worn
People ask, but can't figure out what she's searching for
She's tried to explain that it's something only she can find
She says *you see, when you loose yourself,*
You can't turn back time
Lost are the days she felt free and alive,
Now she waits until the stroke of five
An indicator to try and forget her pain,
She knows it's wrong and wants to refrain
She wants to get back to her past days,
Where it was clear and never clouded in haze
She's tried to look for what she'd lost years ago,
But someone was always there to reinforce the word *no*
She stared at herself straight in the mirror,
Yelled, screamed, flipped up her finger
She took a big step into the universe,
Refusing to make her parents watch her leave in a hearse
She sought out help and began a new journey,
She was shit scared but it was better than ending up on a gurney
The leaves crinkle beneath her feet,
She stops at a park bench to take a seat
She won't find her charm right away
That she knows
But she knows she will find it again one day

This Pity

I try to be motivated
By the simplest of things
But nothing brings a flood of water
To the desert springs

So fuel me up with hatred
And set fire to my bed
Fill me up with kindness
Make a flower crown for my head

If I could write a million words per minute
I'd be
In a world full of fantastic illusions
If I could find a source of determination
Then
I'd be fine

I try to be motivated
By the simplest of things
But you can't force a dry riverbed
To rush water to these springs

Goddess

It's easy to blame someone when your heart is broken
But I've learned that love is a two way street
Among everything else in this world
Perhaps we were still learning how to love another without limits
Like they were the best thing in the world
All the while trying to do the same for ourselves
So today I'll forgive you for breaking my heart the way you did
I will say I am sorry too,
For not loving you the way maybe I was meant to

This Pity

She gave you all her love even when you didn't give her yours
She gave you her warmth
She sheltered you from that breeze you found too cold
She was your rock when you needed to be a waterfall
And she was the one who cried to keep you strong
She was all the things you never saw but still she kept on being
And just like **Mother Nature**
I will tell you
She will take it all back someday

You watched your world burn
It was no longer a song of the past
You sung but didn't feel
For now the world divides
And I swear you can hear
Her cry
If you listen to the winds stories
Of all that man have done

-Mother Earth please forgive us

My palms kiss the sky
A burning flicker in our eyes
And I can't help but wonder
If this is for a season
Or forever

-goodbye my dearest

And I'm still not sure
If it's better to hurt after it all
Or during

You should know that you deserve
More than the guy who won't text you back
The person who can't seem to make time for you
The tears you try to hold back for the one you swore you didn't like
Who left you alone
All the empty promises you tried not to get excited for
All the hopes that never stood true to be
You deserve more than that feeling of hurt

Darling you do, and so do I

I'm not gonna fix you
You're not broke
You say that's all I see in you
That I should move on
And give up hope
That one day I'll heal you
But I'll say it
And I'll say it again
I'm not gonna fix you
You're not broke
Though your edges may be torn
And you may have parts that need patching
They're not mine to mend
They're mine to admire

So, my dearest
I'm not gonna fix you
You're not broke
You're someone who's gone through it
And through it again
But I'm not gonna fix you
Oh my darling,
You are not broke

-I hope one day you can feel whole again

Perhaps I didn't love him in some of the ways I should have
Loved him in patience
Loved him with more heart
So to him, I am sorry
But I realized
I didn't love myself in the ways I should have either
I didn't put her first
I didn't love her in patience
Or with much heart
And so to her, most of all
I am sorry too

He wanted me to be his peace
But I didn't understand
How I could be his peace
When I couldn't be my own
For years of destruction
Can rip away any peace that used to reside

This Pity

How does it feel
To be wrapped up in a strangers arms
To feel their fingers through that hair of yours
To feel the touch of fingers on skin
To feel sad that they do not know you
Like you want them to
Darling,
Give yourself a hug
Get to know yourself

-My heart hurts knowing you are a stranger to yourself

Goddess

He ripped out my wings
And then punished me
Because I didn't know how to fly

He took care of me
But he was lying
He didn't want me to leave him

How can that be
He said he'd always love me
Time it heals, you will find
But you can't heal if the past ain't behind

He put me on a leash
Said I'd never be free
For I gave him my promise long ago

My skins still pretty
My heart and head are weak
Can you really blame me

Here's your chains
Here's your hatred
Here's all the love you never gave
Let me leave
Or I will find a way
If a fights you want
Here's a fight you won't forget

How can that be
He said he'd always love me
Time it heals, you will find

So I'll be healing with my past behind

And if you look at a person
Deeply into them
You will see the good in them
The part of them they buried away from the world
So they wouldn't lose it
Though you will find
Some of us have bad memories
And forgot where we hid them within ourselves

Goddess

He once called me his light
But after a while I realized that
I wasn't his sun
And he wasn't my plant
He needed to grow on his own

What am I fighting for?
It's always me fighting for someone
Never the other way around
Why should I fight for you when you can't do the same
What am I doing?
Why am I fighting for you?
Why am I always the fighter?
When I always thought
I was the lover

You still remember that?

Yes

Why?

Because you stripped every part of me away when you said that. And in that moment I think you lost me before either one of us knew you did

-seeing the stranger you used to call more than that

This Pity

And I cried tears

-words the heart can't explain

And you twirl away from them
Your body spinning like a dance for the last time
You arms bent until they straighten out
And you separate from each other
Fingers unlocking to free the space between
And it's almost like you hear them whisper
Don't find yourself a better life
Not just yet
For you can feel the pain
Seeping through their pores
And you bet they can sense yours too

And perhaps those that tell you
That being single
Is something to not be proud of
Have never found the comfort in their own arms
Perhaps they have never seen
How completely content and happy you can become
When you are alone
For just because you are alone
Does not mean you are lonely
And maybe they never gave themselves the chance
To know themselves better
Which is heartbreaking
Because being in a relationship
But not being able to understand your own soul
I'd imagine
Is painful
Especially when you don't understand why you don't feel whole
Since there's a breath that sleeps beside you

Goddess

Listen to me speak the same words as you
But listen to the difference in my
Pronunciation
Because when *I'm sorry* escapes my mouth
It actually means something

I wanted you to be the one I'd choose over anyone else
Over anything else
But I couldn't
As hard as I tried I found myself letting me down
I'd choose everyone else over myself
And now I see that that's the worst betrayal of all
I was more loyal to everyone else
Than my actual self
That I betrayed my soul
And let my mind swallow my feelings whole

Every time

Why, look at yourself there
Standing in the mirror
Picking apart the parts of you
You should be proud to love
For those lines and dimples
Show that you're human
And I wish I could convince you
You don't always need to try so hard
You could just *be*

This Pity

Even the most strong and powerful women
Need to be held every now and again
To crumble and hurt
To feel what the body demands to be felt
So don't be embarrassed
When the arms that catch you
Aren't your own

Such a strong woman
Done so wrong
I wish she would understand
That if she crumpled
I'd catch her

I hear the creeks of her old floorboards
And the humming of a forgotten story
Honey, I'm listening I whisper
I wrap my arms around her and speak
You are safe here
I am listening
Let me understand what you try to tell me
I hear the door unlock
I feel my heart open
And I become drenched in a waterfall of lost emotions

And I feel my arms catch myself

Goddess

I could never look at you and tell you with words
How you aren't enough
I can't tell you with pinches of skin
With slaps to your flab
I can't look at you and tell you
With crooked lips and sideways eyebrows
How you're not enough for me
So why can I tell myself that everyday
In every way that can be cruel

-Things I need to change

It isn't in the way you fall to the floor
As a monsoon erupts from your eyes
Or how you fall to your knees
With begging pouring out of your lips
It is in the way those eyes of yours sink
When the sockets can no longer hold them
And you can see through those windows and find
There is no fight left inside those tired eyes

-defeated

She paints on her freckles
While *she* covers them up
She straightens her hair
And *she* curls it up, nice and big
Those girls get tans
And that group over there?
They buy skin paling masks

He shaves his beard twice a week
And *he* buys growth serum
He drinks weight gaining shakes
While *he* gulps weight loss juice
He suppresses his tears
And *he* wishes he had a drop to shed

Why oh why
Do we spin around our lust
And love everyone else but our own
Wishing and trying to be what we are not
When in fact
We should embrace all that we are
Without apologizing for all the love we give ourselves

And the day you learn how to love unselfishly
You will never understand the greatness of all love is
Because anyone can feel it when they love someone and are loved back
But when you love someone
And you feel them slip out of love with you
You are left with such destruction
But my dear
If you can still love that person as dearly as the day before they left
Even when you know it is unrequited
That is real
That is raw
That's how you know you are capable of love
Even when the fire it gives off is burning the rib cage that holds it

-To see the beauty in the destructed

Goddess

Won't you sip from my flask
And tell me I am welcome here
Tell me how you aren't afraid
For I was never someone that would hurt you
But still this burden is laid upon my chest
An iron mesh suit I feel guilty for
For my people have
Stolen the things you will never get back
And all I can do is speak softly
Try not to speak a cliche
Be gentle and patient
And never hurt you
For I can understand how
Someone taller
Perhaps stronger
Can be daunting
For Satan can also dress up
And they'll say it's your fault
If you ask him to dance

-I wish I could apologize for the ones who have savaged you

This Pity

We will promise you keys of advancement
That only we know you will never be given
We will let you look up at the sunshine
To remind you of the transparency that separates us
Because you are a woman
And I, a man
We will make *funny* remarks
And take offence when you are offended
And we will make sure we teach our daughters and granddaughters
That they need someone who can support them
With Gucci, Chanel and Bentleys
Since we know what lurks behind those chauvanistic locked doors
But the truth is

These lies were built by
Tiny men in big chairs

We are a sad generation
With happy pictures
We show the good
We hide the bad
And it's easy for us to do
Since our screens do more talking than our actual mouths do
We add filters to showcase the fake
And beam at our *flawless* those strangers comment on
We take hundreds of photos to get the best
And delete the rest to show how good we get
We post a sunny, smiley throwback when we are sad
In hopes of ditching our lonely sadness for a moment
We revolve around likes, like itès something to be proud of
Such a shame we can't love ourselves without
The taste of attention and reassurance
Someone tapped your picture because you were happy
And you were smiling
And they too, want to find that
For they're happiness is worth finding
All because
We are a *sad generation*
With *happy pictures*

And
It never was a scary word
Until you hear her coupled up
In the most unforgiving way
Loved *and* lost
Tried *and* failed
Strength *and* pain
Find *and* replace

-*And* you will need her

Sorry
He said
Time
And time again
As if it were his magic eraser

-your magic doesn't work on me anymore

And when we said
I love you more
My eyes
And my lips
Were the only ones
That weren't lying

You're eyes are brown
But to me they're blue
Just as sadness is seen by the ones who have felt it

Find what hurts
And rock the cradle
Sing it sweet notes of I love you's
Until it's salted water is stable

Hug it hard and hug it long
And hold it's hand until it's strong
Strong enough to not be known as hurt
And enough to be called free

So find what hurts
And pay it some attention
Because once you heal
You understand the lesson

Don't be scared to lend out your hand
And give yourself the love
Your body craves for you to understand
Open your ears and clear your mind
So tell me my love
What do you need to not feel sad?

-The questions my body carves out for my mind

Goddess

I wish you didn't break all of your promises
And I wish I loved you like I used too
When I was young
With glitter in my eyes
The world spread out before me
Before I heard all of their stories
Of what would make me *worthy*

-Dear little me

You say it feels like I don't need you
Like I never do
Because I'm *too strong*
Too independent
And *too enough*, for you

Though you were wrong
For just because I may be those things
Does not mean I don't need you
That I do not want you
I want to be these things alongside you

And I knew
That it's not your job to make me feel like a woman
It never was
And I realized
It was never my job to make you feel like a man

-don't put that blame on me

You loved her
You left her
You hurt her
You forgot her
And now you want her sympathy?

Pity

This Pity

Ah yes
Meant to
Hold her
Meant to
Love her
Always

Always
Meant to
But
Meant to
Is not
What is

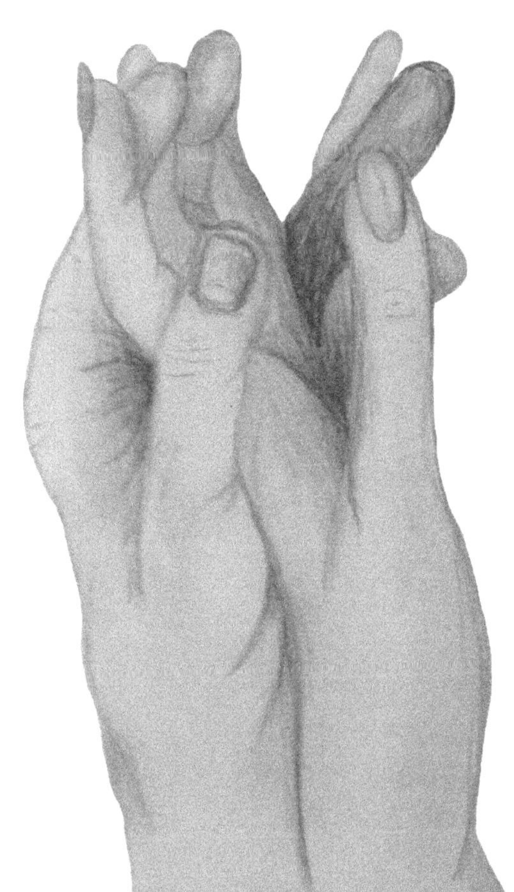

THIS GLORY

Goddess

I had love
And then I lost it
And after a while
It returned to me
But this time it was different
It was sacred
It was a love that I wasn't scared to lose
For I saw this love
When I stared into the mirror
And she came home to me

This Glory

Excuse me, you are in my way
May I pass?
No problem, if you will not move
It makes the journey more fun
I will go around
Or I will climb over you
And maybe I'll need to slip under you
Either way, I will get around
And my victories will taste far more sweeter

Goddess

Hold
Out your palms
And trace the lines that are there
They'll tell
Your story
Even when you're scared
For they will give away your traits
And those who read them
Will follow your lines
But just like those ripples
On your skin
You're never ahead
You're never behind
You're always on time

This Glory

She became the light
They said could never be found
For she grew tired of waiting
And she knew she was capable
Of more than what they allowed her to be
So she strapped on her love
And opened her heart
And she was everything
They were scared she would be
She was set *free*

Kiss my lips
And taste how I love you
But also feel how I do not need you to know love
So kiss my lips and taste our romance
Know how much I love you
But know
I will walk away if I need to

He said
Captivate me with your beauty
So I put on my mascara and tinted my lips
And he said
No my dear
Not with *that* beauty
The one inside your head

And how beautiful it is
To be beautiful
Not for the eyes
But
For the soul

The thing is

I love to love
So I will keep loving
Even when I get hurt
Time and time again
I will heal myself with love
And I will love
For the thing is
I love to love

-Oh how I love how I love

You know the kind of ache
The ache where your heart breaks
All over again
Where you feel your hearts pulse yearn for what's no longer there
But there's a different ache
It exists I swear
And you can feel it if you are so lucky to find it
I call it *love-ache*
The kind where you love so strongly and so fiercely
That your heart aches
And it is full of the purest love
It's like honey and flowers and all the most wonderful things
But with a twist
For it has cayenne, perhaps white pepper and some tangy bits too
But I will tell you one things for sure
You may notice when you're in love-ache and once you notice
You know
And you'll be so happy you were able to find something
That gave you this knowing
Even if it's not in your favour

It will always be yours

Kiss me like you imagined you would
Time and time again
Before you had me to call your own
And before I knew your name
Kiss me like you always wanted to
And don't let me forget
How much you love me
And all the reasons why you are the one I choose

Goddess

We lay in the bed
Covered in white sheets
The sun streams through the window
The black
Aged railing outside
Turns to shadows as it creates patterns on the bed
You
Laying half covered by the wispy covers
Me
Laying partially clothed
Sideways in the sun on the quilts
Laughing and smiles
Bed breakfasts
Quiet mornings
Fruit feedings and coffee sipping

-Watch how we say I love you without saying a damn thing

This Glory

Fingertips on skin
And lips on necks
Hands on thighs
And hearts on chests

I gave you my soul
Before I gave you my body
I gave you my key
You kept it safe until I was ready

Breakfast on balconies
And coffee in sheets
Kisses in rain
And blushes pinned to my cheeks

You're a gentleman, tried and true
A handsome face and a handsome mind
How could I be this lucky
I get to call you all mine

It is not taken
It cannot be stolen
You can only get it
Once it's given

-Love

Start by kisses to my fingers
And next
The arms
Make your way up to my neck
But don't stop there
Kiss my cheeks
And then my forehead
And finally
Kiss my lips
Take the road as curvy as it may be
To get to them
But please
Just start

If you are wanting to find a love
Just to love and feel the merging of two souls
This is a wonderful thing
If you are afraid of being alone
Then this is *the very reason you need to be*

-long for *love* not the fear of never finding it

This Glory

And I will love you
For a long time
And even when you think I don't just know that I do
And I know it's hard sometimes
You wanna break down
Even if I'm not around just know that I'm with you
And I know your streams sometimes
They turn into rivers
And when the waters start crashing you fear you'll drown

I'll hold you in my arms tonight I'll let you know that it's alright
You don't have to have it all figured out
And when the daylights gone and you can't carry on
Let the moon catch you and wrap you up
Just to whisper that you're enough

And I can see it there
At the end of your tunnel
If you can't see the light hold my hand and I'll guide you
I hope you know you're strong
Even when the earth shakes you
Cause I know when you fall you'll get up again
And I hope you know you're loved
Feel my heart pounding
My words could never express just how much I love you

I'll hold you in my arms tonight I'll let you know that it's alright
You don't have to have it all figured out
And when the daylights gone and you can't carry on
Let the moon catch you and wrap you up
Just to whisper that you're enough

Thank you
Thank you for showing me I could banish spiders all by myself
For encouraging me to go for a dream few knew about
For giving me a way to rise above what I thought I knew
For letting me grow
For accepting me as I was and am
For anticipating the days I reached new heights
For finding a way to let me see myself as I should have all along
For cultivating the idea
That I am capable of so much more than I knew and know
For expressing those words of goodbye
For learning that I'm better off without
And *thank you for leaving*

-for I may never have found out how truly magnificent I am if you had
stayed

Sometimes the words that hit us the hardest are the sad ones
The ones that rock you
The ones that leave craters behind that you swear can't be fixed
But what if
The words that move us are simple
Simple in the ways beauty is found in life
The sparkle of the water as the memories of rocks skip it's surface
The way her smile lights up as her hair is tousled in the wind
A golden halo of rays that kiss her silhouette
The laughter of children in a park humming the lullabies of birds
The delight of the words *I love you* and *you are indeed beautiful*

What if these simple moments and words were the ones that lingered
Instead of the hard ones
What an extraordinary idea that could be

-perhaps because of these hard times, we understand what it is to be
happy

I will not complain
Pain makes me stronger
Love makes me more knowledgeable
So I will take all these pieces
And I will harness my energy
And I will be the woman my heart always wanted me to be

This Glory

Oh my
To see a woman
And another woman
Watering eachother
What a spectical with all it's grandness
For I have seen
Hate and jelousy
And all the worst things
Come between
Two ladies
When all they searched for was acceptance
But now we have ate
At eachothers tables
And cleaned the spoons
Of the ones that fed us
And we realised
We only ever wanted
To accept ourselves

Goddess

Come and sit with me my dears
Let us drink wine
And gossip about our
Untold romances
For we share a sisterhood
Of Pinot Grigio
And the shoulders of the ones
Who can understand

This Glory

The wells of my eyes began to fill with salt water
My cheeks felt the rain
This time though
The rain wasn't from grey skies and cloudy views
It was from blooming flowers
And the love I found within myself
Here
I found myself completely happy

-Truly, one hundred percent

I'm a lot to love
I know
But
I love a lot too

I stayed
And it hurt me
I stayed and my mentality payed the price
I stayed as I inhaled the fumes of toxicity
I stayed and watched my light decay
I stayed for too long
But
I don't stay anymore
I leave
I leave behind what has gone
And I have shifted
For I'd rather be
Happy and glowing
Then sacrifice my soul
Ever again

And I hold my hand and
Revel in that glory

Look at that sunset
There is one for every day
Though they will never be the same
So beautiful, each of them
In their own way
The sun will rise to fall
And will fall to rise
Glowing more perfect each and every time

She is gold
And she is yellow
She is pink
And she is violet
And each one melds their colours together to create a perfect pallet

They become old
They were once new
With freshly painted skylines
Some, you don't get to see all the time
They change even as the world turns
Perhaps this was the cause for them to morph

So watch her change as the night is quenched of life
And hold her hand as if you'll never see her again
After all,
I am only speaking of a mere sunset

This Glory

My dears
Tell me you won't forget
That even when you feel broken or half of a something
You are whole
For when parts of the moon are hidden away
And unseen by all
They are still full
Their secrets hidden away
Their craters hiding to heal themselves
But when they reveal themselves again
You understand why they were hiding
And a grand solstice to present their glory
Will come again
If you have the vibrancy to see it

Goddess

I hope you found all the love I gave to you
In an old brown box you put it into
I know you burried it seven feet in the ground
I hope you found it and pulled it all out

I'm not writing these words for you to come back
Or to hurt your heart and make you feel bad for leaving
I just want to make sure you found what it was
You needed
So so long ago you left searching to find it

So I hope you gave the love I gave to you
To someone else
To someone else who needed it
And I hope you kept some of the love I gave to you in your pocket
And hold it tight on the days you really need to feel it

And how can I love them even when they hurt me
When they make me sad
Why do I feel a love burning for them
In my heart
Like the sweetest song you've ever heard
Perhaps because I know what it is to be broken
To know how it feels
When love flows away from you
Like all the pieces of you are trickling away down a stream
And perhaps I love a love even when it hurts because
I know where pain resides
I know where it lingers and where it demands to be known
I have been broken
So forgive me when I love you unconditionally
Because I know what it's like to feel the light on my skin
And I know what it's like to feel a glimpse
Of a shine in someone else's eyes

-I hope you can see the love in my eyes and I hope you can feel your
shine

Goddess

I never tell the sunset to dull down her bright colours
Or to meld them more perfectly
I would never tell a sunset that she isn't beautiful enough
Or that she'd be more beautiful if she had a different shade of purple
You are the sunrise and the sunset
And I would never tell you those things
For I simply admire and love you for what you are
Beautifully beautiful

This Glory

And she grows
Even on the days there are clouds
For she knows
That soon it will return
And a fool she'd be
If she didn't think the rain
Could help her bloom

Goddess

Oh glorious sun
How I look up to you
How you make me blush
How you make me beg
To be touched by your warm rays
For you are so sweet
And affectionate
And know I will grow
If I am shown warmth
And love

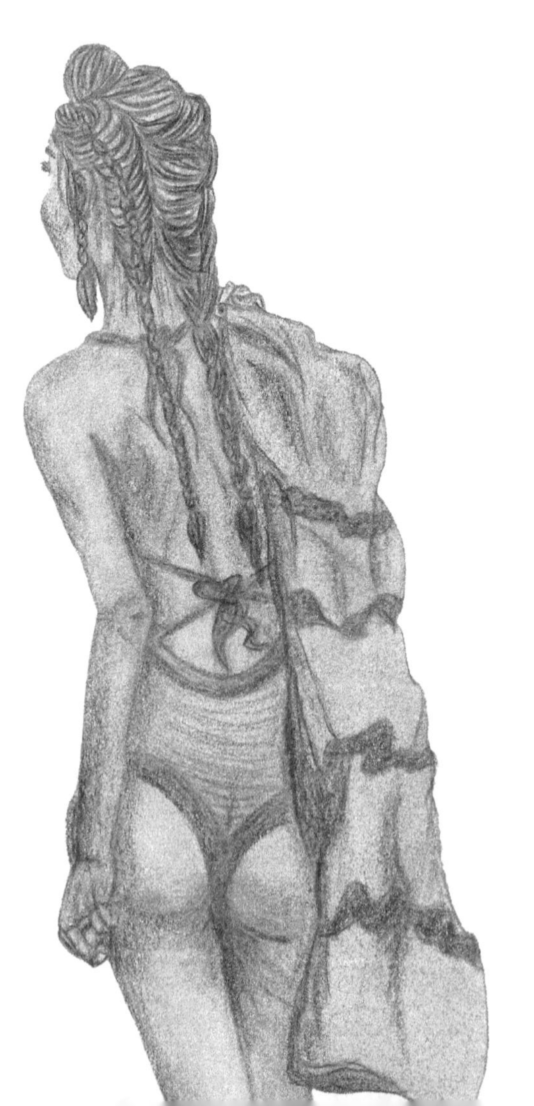

This Glory

Can you name one sweeter
A kiss on the lips
Or the forehead in bed
A hug so tight
You never worry it will end
And a thought so sweet
You can't help but
Just let it sink in

And I will count the ways
You love me
For you may not have always
Been so sweet
So kind
And so gentle to me
But I know
You were figuring out how
All these years
And I am so glad
That today
You looked in the mirror
And whispered
I love you
One thousand times
And more

When they say you are *unlovable*
Or that you are not a feast for the eyes
Perhaps they have a shaky mind
Since I know that those are the ones
Who believe these things to be true
Not about you
But about *themselves*
And if instead we
Return kindness to them
Instead of pistol comments
They wouldn't cry themselves to sleep
For they'd be given seeds
And they'd be busy
Planting their own gardens

Take a look inside my hands
For I am holding it tightly
But if you ask nicely
I may be able to slip you a peak
Through my pinky or thumb
What's that you ask?
Why
It's my blood
Sweat
Tears
And glory

Hallelujah
They sang
As if an alter choir
Echoed from above
For they finally found
Themselves
And well
That's worth something
Something priceless

Sweet pea
Please tell me that you know
How the rain aches to tap on your skin
How the sun begs to give you a golden kiss
How the snow hopes to fall upon your soft tongue
How the trees lean in your direction
And tell me that you know
How those winds
They do dare to sweep across your supple skin
For they know
You are worth knowing

This Glory

I cut my hair
Just to change myself
My neighbors
How they stare
I don't mind them judging
For I feel different
Weightless in my fears
I used scissors to cut the damage
And as those locks fell to the floor
As if in slow motion
To ignite a belly full of laughter
Light and love
I cut my hair
Just to change myself
I like who
I am becoming

And I don't mind if they don't

Goddess

This constellation
Upon your skin
As I run my fingers
Along your face
To connect the dots
You've never loved
Your canvas
A night sky
With supernova eyes
A beautiful galaxy
Made up by stunning freckles
And lit up eyes

Did you love me
Like you said you loved me
Before you broke me
And left me down in pieces
I used to ask you
If you loved me
Like I loved you
Because I guess I never believed you
When you said you do
And I cried tears that only god knew fell
And picked myself up off that ground
And I stitched my soul back together stronger
And now even though you're gone
I still smile
For I don't care if you loved or love me
Because *I love myself*

Tianna
A lavender aura
Screaming out her goodness
For she would give you her soul
If it meant you wouldn't bleed
And you hear her words caress your name
As she speaks to you a simple phrase
You needn't ask her for help
For she will look into your eyes
And know
Lasso your heart
And pump it red again

She smells like raspberries
But I'll bet she tastes
Like strawberries
For she is only sweet
Not sour at all

Goddess

And when you meet her
You will know
For she will have
A beautiful smile
Gorgeous light filled eyes
Full luscious lips
And you will
Only see her soul

And in those open arms
You will find her heart
For she does not bury it away
She pins it to her sleeve or her blouse
And marches forward straight
In her eyes of trying times
Her tears they run away
For when they're dry
They long for her to know
The magic of her ways
How she can laugh
And turn pain to freedom
For when she smiles
You're sure to know
That's my dearest Lisa

And she will love you
And you will know when
For it will be winter
And she will forget
Her sweater

This Glory

Those clouds
They do move for you
Parting ways to sky
So the sun could shine
Upon your vivacious locks
And make love to your rosy cheeks

Goddess

Can you string me a line of sweet sentences
I want to taste those thoughtful words
As if you were whispering lullabies in my ears
To not think about if you mean them or not
Just to let those words flow into my ears
And kiss my mind
To feel sweet as if sprinkled in gleaming pearls of sugar
As I watch these butterflies land on me

Did you hear
The way she sung
I love you
Like a song strung out of
Perfect lines
And perfect cords too
A gleam in her eyes
You knew were green
But blue
In the ways she once sung
His name
Some would say it was a song for hurting
But there were no tears
Just a dew drop upon her iris
And that is a sign
Of the purest love
When it is being reminisced

Goddess

White as snow
With sun burnt lips
How they make the most beautiful contrast

Pale with freckles
A beautiful human constellation
Why, wouldn't you get lost in those stars

Yellow like the sun kissed her cheeks
Thin eyes when she smiles
But just look at how her love and light pours out those dainty crevasses

A caramel kiss with sparkling dark features
She, I'll bet
Is a fiery lady with deep passions

Brown and beautiful
Look at the way she moves
With perfect pace
Just as she was meant for this earth

Skin as black as the night
And oh how it glows
Like moonlight on a perfect ocean

And instead of venomous words
They spit
Love and upliftment
Grabbing at each other's hands
Basking in each of their glories

Inhaling their breaths
Hearing those words
And feeling each heartbeat

This Glory

I found you
I found you
And I'm so glad I did
You see
I was searching to find her
For so many moments
But as I stepped out of my boots
I revealed my toes
And as I unraveled my clothing
My nakedness froze
It is me
It is I that stands here
Oh boy
I must have covered her up
With all the things that don't belong

I promise
I won't hold you back

For doing such a disservice
Would be a complete waste
Of the magnificence you are

And she kissed me
But I never tasted her lips
I tasted the life between them
And the things she holds true
I tasted
Her love
Her loyalty
Her time
Her trust
And it was the best thing
I had ever swilled

THIS
LAUGHTER

And when she smiles
Well
You'll know when she does
For the sun awakens just to kiss her good morning

This Laughter

Ah the fickle moon
He appears to me
Just to entice my howl
To hear my happiness escape
And he always wins
For, for him
I will always reveal my laughter

Goddess

Oh I am not
An easy thing to love
But may the sun make me soft
And the moon keep me full

And time is such a fickle thing my dear
A flower can lie dormant for years
But when it blooms
Oh, how it blooms
Just like a person can one day explode
With self love

And never look back

Sweet soul
Remember that
You have always been
The person that you are afraid to be
So don't put her at bay
Embrace her
Revel in her
Let her consume you
Because the person that you are afraid to be
She is you
She always has been

And to those who know exactly who you are
I am so happy for you
So happy you had the wonderful chance of exploring all that you are
So you could understand the way you tick
And the way you *become* in the moment
But maybe
It would also be wonderful if you could see how some of us
Need a bit longer
To learn about what we are to ourselves
To learn not only about what we want to do with our lives
But to learn
What makes us laugh
What makes us cry and scream to the dear lord
What makes us crumble and how we can put ourselves back together
For it's not a bad thing to know who you are
In fact it's marvellous
So maybe
It's not a bad thing if we don't know who we are yet either
Perhaps it's alright if all we know
Is that we love to feel the sun on our skin
And to
Run and hide behind drying sheets as the winds brush our hair for us
Because maybe just *being* is enough

-maybe for now

Goddess

He uttered to her long before she cared to ask
I will be full and fine as long as you remember me
And if you do
Well
I wouldn't mind if everyone else forgets

This Laughter

He woke up
Hair a complete mess
She awoke next
Her smile
The sweetest
She kissed his laugh
And ruffled his war-torn hair

Dark hair
Strong bones
Words of laughter where wisdom shows
An earthly spirit
Contained soul
One that is let free
When you call it home
You may see her
And never know
The technical fluidity
Of how her blood flows
But you will know her
And she is
Sweetly Miranda

The crashing waves
The vast wilderness
The universe
You

Isn't it wonderfully incredible how something can be so completely
beautiful, yet so utterly terrifying?

And when you lay
In the dirt
In the middle of a storm
You can hear the winds usher the trees
To tell you all their secrets

This Laughter

I sat in the grass
I watched the reeds
A smile swept my face
For I know how they bend with the skies
Just to kiss the lake
Goodnight

Cayenne painted
Setting skies
Let me kiss you before the night
Before your colours lay to rest
And turn into complete blackness
A muddled mess
Dark like pepper
Sprinkled with salt
Although
It's burning stars make me halt
Cayenne painted
Setting skies
Let me watch you again
Tomorrow night

Head out the window
Close your eyes
Listen to the wind tell you
It's secrets
And hear the laughter in your hair
As they dance amongst existing

Goddess

You love when you see those dimples of hers
So won't you tell me mine are beautiful too?
The ones on my thighs
They're covered in them
Perhaps because I smile
When I look at my body in the mirror

This Laughter

Butterfly's on her eyes
Lady bugs on her cheeks
Rose buds on her lips
Oh can you hear her sing?!

And I'll dance by the fire
And laugh with all my beautifully lit flames
By myself
Until someone can love me
And all my fire
While I burn

And that night
I danced with the winds
I heard the grasses play alongside the crickets harmonies
I swayed to the frogs orchestras
And
That night
Under the moonlight
I knew what it meant to be heard
Even in the dark

Live deep enough
To feel the rain
Breathe in the cold morning air
Taste the sun
Dance with the wind
Live deep enough that you know you're *alive*

This Laughter

Dear night
How you cloak glory with fear
I will never know how effortlessly it comes to you
My vision impaired
For what was beautiful moments ago
Is now foreign to me
I am accompanied only by 3
Scent, touch and my strained hearing
So will you hold my hand
And teach me to move confidently amongst the dark?
For you are so strong and courageous
And perhaps
You could wait with me until morning

-to find comfort in complete darkness

Goddess

Oh glorious sun
Beat down on my skin
And kiss it like the moon
Leave me golden
And present a halo around my bronzed freckles
As if I've felt this dewy and glowing movement
Every day

This Laughter

Watch her twirl
Her flowy dress
Creating patterns
Her hair a mess
A sun kissed smile
And sun kissed skin
Daisies in her hair
Golden air caressed
By her face in the wind
Lace details on her dress
She falls to the ground
Her body a giggling mess

Oh dearest wind
Take me away
In the breeze
Let me fly
Above the clouds
As if to know what it is to
Feel weightless

This Laughter

Hear her howl
As the moon appears
Full and bright
And those doubters
And disbelievers
Are shaken back into their hallow homes
For they swore
She would be silenced
When the darkness came

Sarah
That wild heart
You'd beat to hear
From a distance
Or from right beside
For she is sure to bring a smile
If you are whole
Or if you are broken
And she will laugh with you
Your name
Until you feel
Whole again

This Laughter

And oh my dear
When he comes back into your life
Please remember the way he left
Before you open your soul
And let him hear your laugh again

Goddess

You conceal your beauty
As if wanting to shield it from the world
When the light hits you though
It shows what you keep under the surface

Hazel eyes

This Laughter

Hear the violin as it so effortlessly turns a written note
Into a dance for the ears
And watch as she taps her two fingers upon the table
One by one
Back and forth
Her gaze never missing a beat
Laughing along with the melody
Without realizing my surprise
For forgetting
How such a small
Seemingly minuscule thing
Can radiate such life and love and laughter
For it is these easy moments
That are taken for granted
But should be cherished

So let's laugh as we listen to the violin perform for us
And we'll tap our fingers and perhaps
Move our feet
To sway with the cords
As if this moments all we have

They ask me about my job
They ask me about my relationships
They ask me where I've been
And where I'm going
If I'm ready to settle down
Or to start a new life somewhere brilliant
But I've never heard the question
Are you happy?
Pour out of their dainty lips
And after all
Isn't that the most important one?

Your mouth was a whipping hand
Your words
A stone
She was the calm
Glassy water
And well
You know what happens
When your stone makes
The perfect skip

She climbs high
Up the sequoia
And she listens carefully
As the stars repeat her dreams
The sky soaks up all her excitement
And the moon
Moves the galaxies
To bring her dreams closer
They all work harmoniously together
To create perfect timing
And bring manifestation to life

Oh to to be a wildflower
For they don't worry about
Where they will grow
Or when
They simply root
And climb with the sun
And then
They sway amongst the winds

Look at those lines
Upon her face
Etched into her skin
Youth escapes her
Time resides
But more than anything
They remain
Her laughter lines

Oh my buttercup
If you hold it under your chin
And you glow
You don't just like butter
You are kissed golden
And sweetly beautiful

Goddess

She smells of pine
And the cleanest dirt
Waterfall hair
Sunshine skin
Rose tinted cheeks
And rose tinted lips
She has the stars in her eyes
The moon in her laugh
And the warmth of the sun in her heart
For she
Is made from earth

Do you hear that laugh
And those clapping hands
Sunlit eyes
And calm like the sands
Wild like the oceans
And smooth like a breeze
You hear her coming
Like timbering trees
But
Do you hear that laugh
And those clapping hands
They say it's *cheyenne's*

Goddess

Tantalizing voice
Even more so her laugh
For when she starts giggling
You can't help but join

Shade me from the sun
It's become too bright up here
I have climbed and climbed
But I fear I've come too high
For it is lonely here
At the top
Although, I must say
I'd hate to retreat
For I would lose my freckles
My sun kissed skin
And my mind

Goddess

The leaves rub against one another
And crackle in the breeze
While the grasses whistle
And tickle the feet that pass
As if laughing at how naïve we are
To believe we are free

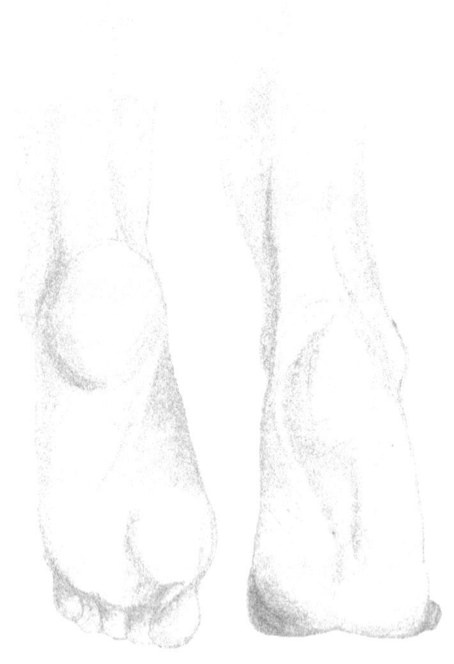

This Laughter

You wonder what feeling alive is?
It's that feeling you get that makes your heart sing
Your mind dance
And makes your whole body echo with the frequency of the universe
Trust in it
Feel it

It's between the crying
And the breaking
And the fake smiles we're all making
It's between the lightly dusted words
And the ones that actually mean something
It's between the things everyone expects to hear
And between the person they take you to be
It's between
If they could see
That the in between is where they'd find you
Where you're meant to be

I tilted my head back
And opened my mouth
Laughter tumbled out of my belly
And trickled up my throat
And out flew millions of fireflies
A sound so sweet and full of life
You could see the light

Goddess

Slit my eyelids open with a razor
So that I can see all the beauty this world has to offer
Peel back my lids
For they hide the light that my irises beg to find
Let me see all the beauty I'm sure there is still to be seen

This Laughter

Even when the rain pours down
She finds the sweetest sentences
And looks for the best in the sky
Because she knows that without the rain
We could never smell the sweet nectar
Of those brightly blooming flowers
Or hear the soft buzzing of the bees
That do their best to sprinkle love
Across the plants that need some

Lightning crashes
Across these summer lit skies
And we can only watch in awe
Of the moment that passes
As the clouds get in formation
To cloak these golden colours that set
The winds pick up
And we can laugh as it tousles our golden hair
The skies perform as if just for us
Thunder shakes the ground
And claps for the lights
That illuminate our bronzed skin
And we can only say *thank you*
By tilting our heads up to the heavens
To taste the rain
As it pours down on our skin
That begs to be touched by nature

This Laughter

She had flowers braided in her hair
And a buttercup glow about her
Her voice was smooth like a silent waterfall
And her laughter
A warm breeze from a summer storm
She had steps so gentle
You'd say she walks on air
And beautifully tinted lips
As if she kisses those tulips goodnight
Have you met her?
The wind will whisper her name
When you call her
And you will hear
Morgan

She said she had a wildflower
One for everyday of loving her
To date she has 7354
For there were years in between
This love
Where it was scarce
For those glossy pages groped her eyes
And those words maced her mind
And since then she's realised
That she deserved a meadow of wilds
That no one could have the power
To take away
By simply implying
She wasn't enough

This Laughter

And she lays there
Peacefully
With butterflies balancing on her face
And the monarch knows
Her finger is a safe place to land
For she sings to the trees
To watch them dance
And she laughs with the winds
That tumble about her perfectly woven hair

Goddess

Take me to the mountain side
Oh please
Won't you take me there
Where the earth is calm
And the trees do bend
And if you climb high enough
You can swallow your fears whole
And taste your dreams
As you look upon
A ravishing sunset

This Laughter

Oh my
How you do weep
For the person
You once were
But, my darling
She is at rest
Deep within your bones
And your new skin is shining
And that soul of yours?
Oh my
How it does beat
For you

She came rolling out
To me
Like a sharp breeze
On the most beautiful day
She had dirt on her face
And thorns in her hair
Jeans ripped at the knees
And in all the chaos
I could only see
How those florals
Leaped from her hair
And danced atop hers eyes
Oh and I was done
When I saw her smile

Her eyes they squint
Her lips they grin
Her dimples embed themselves
Into her cheeks
Her lips they open
And her laughter pours out
Her smile is genuine
Her heart beats loud

And when the wind brings the lilies
To leap into your hair
And whisper that you are beautiful
You must believe them

And she will sing for you
Until peace has returned to you
This rock of healing
She opens her geode hands
To reveal a love saved
Just for you
Her child or a stranger
It need not matter the cloth you were born into
For she is gentle and she is kind
And if you are lucky enough to mine her
You will have all the riches in the world
For she isn't a Crystal
That is her name
And oh, how she does sparkle

THIS
STRENGTH

Goodbye to who I used to be
To who I thought I was
Goodbye to all the times I didn't feel like myself
To all the versions of myself people wanted me to be
Goodbye to everything I am not
To everything I am not supposed to be

-unbecoming

And sometimes us girls
Will cut our hair
Some will think we are manic
Having a mental breakdown
But sometimes we are just cutting our hair
To change who we are
At least for a little while
To find the newness within our aging bodies
And perhaps if we were hurting
Well maybe we cut our hair
In hopes of cutting loose
The pain too

Goddess

A rose has thorns
And you have a mind
Sharp and beautiful

This Strength

I see you
Only wanting to give me attention
When I no longer want any from you
You wanting to push back into my life like you
Never left in the beginning
And perhaps you never left in the physical
But when I must beg for you to show me you care
That's when I'm gone
I'm not going to stick beside someone who
Doesn't want to stand by me
Because maybe once upon a time
I needed validation from men like *you*
And way back when
I needed the attention so I didn't feel so alone
But I'm grown and I'm done
And I can wait for as long as I need to
To find the one who isn't going to give me the *lust to leave*

Goddess

You spit your words at me
Thinking you are dirtying my name
You live believing that your words are like venom
Oh honey,
If you could only know that I am like Medusa
And the venom you soak me with is only making me stronger
It is working with me
Not against me

-If you only knew how powerful you are making me

I am a lady
And sometimes I utter things that counteract that statement
Things I wanted to say straight to his face
But because I am a lady
I did not
And now thinking back on that day I wish I had said what I wanted to
Holy shit, he really is a bastard

Goddess

What the hell do you mean by soul food they ask
It is doing what simply makes you happy
Giving your body another reason to keep thriving
To pump the blood through your whole body
To smile once more with even more light than the ones before
To laugh uncontrollably
Wondering if you'll ever stop
It's finding something that feeds you
Something that seizes your hunger when your soul asks for more

-may I have some more

This Strength

And you can tell me how I have what I have because
I simply have it
But maybe you don't know
The sweat and tears and blood
That got me what and where I am
Because you were never the one holding my hand
When I was building it all
You were merely sitting behind the scenes
Hoping I would fail
And now that you're here reaching out for my hand
Don't be offended
When I grab the palms
That were always holding my heart
As I failed

Goddess

The ocean is ready
She will swallow you whole
For she will not let you
Hate on her
As you try and overtake her
The ocean is ready
And she will swallow
Those unappreciations whole

This Strength

You don't get half of me
If you don't want to know all of me

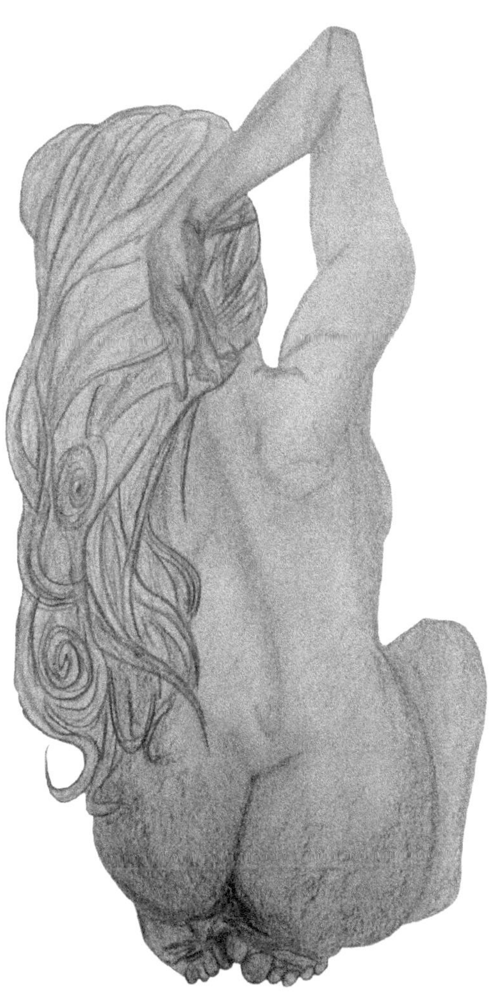

To compare yourself to another
Would be like comparing
A lilac and a geranium
Both are beautiful
Both are different
It doesn't make sense
Completely unnecessary

These bruises
Remind me of my disobedience
But also of my strength
For you chained me
Forced me to follow in your truths
When my truths were different
I am wild and unknown and that's how I like it
So these bruises may be left upon my skin
Upon my mind
But in my heart resides strength
For my bruises were from something that tried to hurt me
But they are no longer here
To wear me down and try it's tyranny
And here I am
I am free

Through the waves
This bliss does ride
Through swirling currents
And rolling tides

This Strength

I used to cage my heart with ice after it had broken
To protect it from the unfrozen storm ahead
Though as I grew
I told myself to not let heartache make me hard
So after years of practise
A slight ice around my heart forms
A frost
And like the temped October morning sun
The frost will melt away with a bit of warmth

-and I will remain soft

Goddess

I hold my hand out for you to take it
I know you wish I could give you more than this
But you dragged me through the dirt too many times
Just know I'm here for you if you wish
We've travelled many miles down this road
My heart never forgets the sights it's seen

I can't love you like I once wished I would
I can't love you like I once know I did
So if you want to be here as my friend
Take my hand and know I will forgive

This Strength

Am I enough?
Enough for you?
I hate that I have to ask you
What you think of me
I wish I knew

I pinch my skin
As I look in the mirror
Always comparing myself to
Those I think are much prettier

I wish I could love myself
The way that you say you love me
One day I love myself
The next, my body has forgotten those gentle words

I tell others that they're perfect
That they're beautiful in their own skin
But then I face myself and beg my mind
To say the gentle words I spoke to them
To myself

Self-love is pure
Self-love is a beautiful thing
Just know I'm trying
Every damn single day
To not say

Am I enough?
Enough for you?
One day I won't have to ask you
What you think of me
Because I'll know

Goddess

I was a storm
I still am
And always will be
I used to think I was the problem
I drove everyone away
Until I met the one who changed it all
I met myself for the first time
I met myself with love
I learned that I am a storm
Not one that you run away from

One that you chase

Rose was her name

Rose was her name and she loved roses
She loved their scent
She loved their thorns
Rose was her name and she loved roses
But she didn't love her thorns

Rose was her name and pricked her thumb one day in the garden
But fell in love even more

Rose was her name and she loved roses
She realized they were for protection
Just like hers must be

Rose was her name and she loved roses
Rose was her name and she knew she was beautifully strong and free

Rose was her name

You tell me to be classy
Not smart-assy
You want me to be calm and quiet
When I am none of those fickle things
Oh my sweet
Domineering man
I am not a mold you try to fit me in
I may be many things you do not desire
So leave me and let me live
Without shackles and sweaty palms
Without sunken eyes and *I am sorry's*
So I can love my soul
Set on fire in all it's glory
This is who I am
And I now
Refuse to say sorry

This Strength

Delicate enough to crumble
Fierce enough to fly
Though strength sometimes escapes you
A quitter would have never tried

Courageous heart you hold
Deep within your shaking bones
You've hurt and healed
And still you grow

I've seen the tears that stain your cheeks
And flow down to those broken feet
It's the salted water that took hold
And saturated your worn limbs to fix your soul

Goddess

Follow your heart they say
I can't say how long I've wanted to
I've wanted to let go of things and
Taken so long to just do them
I've always ended up loving the way it feels
To let go and to live by my heart
So today even though fear is whispering he is here
I am ready to live up to the desires my heart craves
I am ready
And so is my heart
Can you feel my glow?

And when you miss me
Just remember that *I wasn't enough*
I know because you told me
And your words could have cut me open and bled me dry
But they didn't
They scathed me and left me fallen
But I picked myself up with these arms that held me
For I knew and will always know
That *I am*
And will always be

Enough

Oh her soul is on fire
But she does not know
Her red hair
A vision of fight
With rings on her fingers
On her toes
Her nose
And in her hair too
She sways with the drum beats as her skin greets the rain
Eyes closed
Envisioning the most beautiful sky
Eyes open
Wide and deep blue
Freckles so perfect
Da Vinci painted them there
A smile that greets strangers as family
And a heart so open she never wonders when it will close
She is the beauty the world never ceases to find
She is the love the sun begs to touch
She is the power the moon aches to hold
And she is the person she doesn't know she can't wait to meet

This Strength

It's between the aching
Between the breaking
Between the shedding tears
And between the shaking hands

It's between the loud voices
Between the slamming doors
Between the the lip quivers
And between the broken bones

It's between all the moments in life that are anything but appealing

-Here you will find yourself happy

She gets up each day carrying hurt inside her heart
And a sewn smile to her face
Not to be fake but
In hopes of feeling happy again
She's been left behind and forgotten
But still she finds herself each time
Some say it's odd to smile when you're sad
And when it's not truly real
Though she'll say
It's one step closer to the real thing
So each night she'll kiss herself goodnight
And each day she'll wake up and put on her favourite smile

And what do they call her?
A warrior

Her eyes sting from salt
Her lips quiver from blizzards
Her skin turns grey like the clouds
And her bones shake like thunder
But she will snap like lightening
And she will set ablaze to a million wildfires

-And it will return to her

And now when I break
I still cry
Though my tears fall and rest below my eyes
Creating a fresh coat of battle paint
Each tear making up another part of that design
Embedding it's clarity deep within my skin
An invisible bravery
I wear as strength

Breathe

Breathe deep.
In.
Out.

Goddess

Ah my dear
The way you lift you head
After it falls
Reminds me of the tiny sapling
We planted years ago
For I swear I heard it
Grasp the dirt
Inhale deeply
And begin again
Just as you do
When you are uprooted
You grasp the earth
Inhale the best for you
And you reroot

And there is strength
In her tears
Oh how she carries them beautifully
For she has known love and heartache
And she holds them both perfectly
For when those sorrows become her
She lets those wings surround her
And scoop up her fragile heart
As they soak her in all the love
She gave to them

-A sweetheart called Jayme

And she cried all night long
An aching poured from her soul
The type that could be felt by a stranger
And as she sat in her field of floods
Water trickled down her tired skin
And made way for invisable seeds
Beneath the dirt
And they would grow and bloom once more
And show her the power
Of her tears

This Strength

And as you shudder from those fears of yours
That lurk in your mind
And wait to pull the rug from under your dreams
Promise me you will take another step
Move with grace and fire
And a lust in your eyes
For in these moments
Where each step is planted
Strength grows and takes up space
And vigor vanquishes those fears

Goddess

Sweet soul
Remember that
You have always been
The person that you are afraid to be
So don't put her at bay
Embrace her
Revel in her
Let her consume you
Because she is you

She always has been

Those hands aren't dainty
They are tough and rough
And blister torn
Calluses paint your palms
Though still
What you carry
Show those hands are gentle
And soft

Goddess

Down on your knees
Feet without tread
A gasping for air
Survival kicked in
War paint upon your cheeks
Fire and furry inside your eyes
Polished freckles on your nose
Grace tattooed in your mind
Oh my dear
How you think you've fallen
But did you know
You rose?

Kiss my cheeks
Leave behind a trace of you
Let it seep into my skin
And be consumed by my soul
For I'd be honored to be gifted strength
By someone like you

She held my hand
When I was broken
And spoke strong words
Of love and wisdom

I'll hold you like I do love you
And if I do this everyday
For one year
Perhaps by then
This habit will become real
And then I can say
I'll hold you always
Since I love you
And my body
Won't feel like a stranger I'd met
But forgotten the name of

Goddess

And she was bleeding from her muted skin
Her face tired and pale
And eyes that cried for you to love her
But she dipped into her skin
And made rosy cheeks
From the pain she grew
So that you would not feel sorry for her
And perhaps never know
For she only ever wanted you to be happy
And that's all she ever wanted for her too

And my dear
I do hope you learn one day
If it is not known by you now
Of all the things once held by you
The best thing you've ever held
Was *you*

Goddess

And she said to me
Find the thing you'd die for
And live for it
For it's so much better
With you and your love around

This Strength

Tempt me with the hallucinations of your mind
And let me grow accustomed to them
For your mind does wander
And your mind is advanced
In these times
But I will walk with you
For I know what is right
And what is wrong
And I need one moment
To collect my courage and strength
And tie it tightly to my waist
So I can walk with both fists in the air
As we march for change

Are you afraid my dear?
You are allowed to be
For how could they label it
Courage and strength
If you were not terrified at all

Oh and of all the tears that fell
From your beautiful eyes
Know that each one made you stronger
For how could you rise above
If you had never known sadness
And had nothing to rise from
And how could you keep moving
If there was never hurt that lurked in
Your *known*

Can you sing to me again
Like a child cloaked in blankets
For your sweet songs
Bring back monsoon memories
Of love and light
And I could use a hand to guide me to
My stolen strength

This Strength

How dare they tell you
You are weak
For they do not know
The stones you've turned
The miles you cried
Or the very steps that got you here

You are always welcome in my garden of solidity

And in those hours
You know the ones I mean
Where the air is thick
But your brows are clean
No sweat or fears to roll upon them
Just the lies of those
Who did not care to know you
Before they told your
Incorrect story
But you sit there
Still and smiling
For perhaps it's better
To have your story unpublished
So only you can know
What makes your mind tick
And what keeps your heart in beat

Please tell me that you know it's alright to forgive yourself
For all the times you were wrong
For all the times you didn't love you
For the times you believed you weren't worth it
And for the times you didn't leave with grace
Because once you forgive yourself
You can try again

Can you hear those tears of hers fall to the floor
Ah yes
Well
They are only planting her
Deeper into the earth
So she can feel nature
And call for her mother
As she cradles herself to remember
Who she is
Those tears of hers that fall
Are not wasted
They empower her love
To find who she was before she
Was lost
And now
Look into her eyes
And see the strength
That grew from her humble feet

Oh mask maker
You have woven me many
Expressions
Perhaps you could make me one of strength
So I could wear it to my new country
And they will not know I am afraid
And they will not pin my name as weak

*Darling, you have more strength inside you than you even
know*

Goddess

Keep your body strong
Your heart soft
Your eyes bright
Your hair long
Keep your skin supple
Your laugh loud
Your lungs full
Yourself proud
Keep your voice yours
Your song sweet
Your feet light
And never forget
To keep your mind safe

Tell me about the time
You put fear in a bag
And buried it four feet down
So that you could pretend
It did not weigh on you

A thousand and one smiles
All are beautiful
Indeed
But you'll see the difference
In the one that isn't just happy
But is *strong*

This Strength

Dear mumma
Can you paint that strength upon my face too
The way you do it for you?
I'd like to have courage
And a lick of heart too
So crack out those felts of yours
And paint paint paint
For I have yet your laughter lines
Or grinning skin beside my eyes
But oh to be cloaked in wisdom
With strength threaded into your cape

And you reach your hand out to me again
Pretending what was last said has vanished
And assuming I will have forgotten all the pain that was there
Hoping I will forget
My worth
For you
But I will never let go of
All of my deserving
For how can you tell me I'm magnificent
And then try to steal away every part of me
And perhaps my friend
My *I love you* will become *I miss you*
And I will just miss you
But I will love myself
For I know what I deserve
And I will not let you
Try to bury that part of me

-You undervalued me *and this time I left*

This Strength

Come in and sit at my table
Here I will feed you
I fed you at my own table
And you repay me by stealing from
My garden
That is okay
You must have been hungry

Come in and sit at my table
Here I will feed you
I fed you again
After everything you've done
And still
You steal from my garden
The one that I planted
The one I poured my soul into

Come in and sit at my table
Here I will feed you
There is less than before
For my crops have been taken
But I will share with you
For you must be terribly hungry

I fed you again
And I heard the trees whisper
Naïve
For you stole away all of my garden
You even took some seeds

Stay out you are not welcome at my table
I do not feed those who steal from me
And leave my fields dry
Without even a *sorry* running down the stream

Goddess

There's strength in my nakedness
Here
As I stand before the earth
Wondering if I will be
Kissed or forgotten

There is strength
In the way
I stand in my colourful skin
For I have yet to know
What is laid out before me

And yet here I stand
With all of my unknowing
And
In all my
Nakedness

I will
Never
Apologize
For being who I am
And if my authenticity
Makes you

Leave

Well then
Your leaving
Will be my

Blessing

And oh to tell them of how glorious they are
And have them believe me
Have them believe themselves
When it is said that they are great, powerful and sweetly magnificent
To watch the honey drip from their eyes as they cry
Tears of love and happiness and pain
And to hope they know I mean what I say
When I tell them

Honey, you are a

GODDESS

Oh how I've longed to hear these words spoken from the bellies of my souls. How I have waited silently with just their taste reminiscent in my mouth. I have devoured every letter with my tongue and suckled on the sentences you've read. To understand the meaning behind each word and grasp the lessons we fight for. We are those who have given in and given up. We are the ones who whimpered in the coldest nights and shed power tears in the morning. We have waivered and wilted and bloomed and here we are. Ready to take it all back. Grab my hands, the world has waited for this moment and we are ready. Hear the buzzing of what belongs to us grow louder. For it will return to us. And my dears, so will *This Goddess*.